SELLING HOMEMADE PORN

How to Sell Amateur Porn in 2020 and Make a Living

by Mike Triumph

Selling Homemade Porn – How to sell Amateur Porn

All rights reserved.

No part of this book may be reproduced in any form or by any electronic or mechanical means, including information storage and retrieval systems, without written permission from the author, except in the case of a reviewer, who may quote brief passages embodied in critical articles or in a review.

Trademarked names appear throughout this book.

Rather than use a trademark symbol with every occurrence of a trademarked name, names are used in an editorial fashion, with no intention of infringement of the respective owner's trademark.

The information in this book is distributed on an "as is" basis, without warranty.

Although every precaution has been taken in the preparation of this work, neither the author nor the publisher shall have any liability to any person or entity with respect to any loss or damage caused or alleged to be caused directly or indirectly by the information contained in this book.

Enjoy it.

Selling Homemade Porn – How to sell Amateur Porn

Table Of Contents

Now is the time to start earning with homemade porn! There has never been a better time than right now!	2
So how much money can you make if you sell your porn online?	3
Requirements to start selling homemade porn videos online	4
Best sites to sell homemade porn	5
I have a free gift for you all.	10
Will my identity be revealed?	10
How to protect myself from people who steal my content ?	11
Advantages of selling your own adult porn clips/videos/pictures apart from webcam shows	12
Best network/websites for selling adult porn video clips/pic etc?	13
So what kind of content should I make?	14
But how do I actually make the porn videos?	15
Steps to find out what content to make:	16
Now that you've made your video, time to upload it	17

Selling Homemade Porn – How to sell Amateur Porn

While it is generally considered really hard to sell the porn today, I will tell and teach you how to easily sell your homemade porn online and make a living doing so. It does not matter if you are single or a couple, you can do it. I have helped hundreds if not thousands of individual achieve the freedom to work for themselves and you can do it too.

Now is the time to start earning with homemade porn! There has never been a better time than right now!

In 2020 there are so many websites that are making it so easy in selling your porn videos.

With technological advancement and cheap camera equipment's anyone can become an amateur porn producer and start selling porn online to make money. Its really very easy to make good videos and sell them online.

Selling Homemade Porn – How to sell Amateur Porn

So how much money can you make if you sell your porn online?

Giving you an absolute number will be unfair on my part. Why? because there are so many factors that affect how much money you make. But also because it is limitless to earn from the porn business. The market is huge. You can make as little as a few bucks a day to thousands. It all depends on how serious you are and how you hone your skills.

If you read this book, follow the tips and do the work - you can and will make money! Play the long game, the longer you do it, the more followers you get and the more you can sell. Not many starts out making bank the first month, but if you keep doing it, you will thank me when you can quit your day job, lean back and watch the cash roll in.

Here are some of the factors that will decide how much money you can make.

Selling Homemade Porn – How to sell Amateur Porn

- **Do you have a following:** If you are already a registered member as a cam girl or adult model who has a fan following then making (more) money will be very easy. Whereas newbie porn producers will first need to market themselves to find customers.
- **Number of sites you sign up on:** The more sites on which you are present the more money you will make. I see so many girls and adult performers make this same mistake. They just stick with one of their favorite website and leaving all that easy money opportunity. So make sure you sign up on all the networks that I recommend later in this book. So you can get more money from different websites, it also protects you if you get banned or if one of the services close down. You DO NOT want all your eggs in one basket.
- **Marketing yourself:** How well you are marketing yourself and how easily you are driving customers to your profile.
- **Quality of your content:** You do not have to produce professional videos, but you do need to make sure that what you do have a market and that it's reasonable quality.
- **Amount of work you do:** I cannot stress this enough, in the beginning you will see little return on the time you invest. But as you produce more and more clips, spend more time online interacting with people, you will see that you start to generate money even if you aren't doing anything. **When you get to a point where your passive income surpasses your living expenses, you will be truly free.** That feeling is beyond anything I've ever experienced and I wish every single human on this planet could feel it. If you want to get there, you have to do the work. Do not give up, do not quit. If you ever feel like giving up, hit me up and I'll nudge you on. **I want you to make it!**

Selling Homemade Porn – How to sell Amateur Porn

Requirements to start selling homemade porn videos online

The requirements are very simple. But let us go over them just to be sure that we are on the same page so to speak.

- **You need to be 18 years old at-least:** Also anyone else in the video must be at-least 18 years old.
- **Camera to shoot videos:** Although nowadays your mobile phones are also equipped with high quality camera. But if you are serious about making money online in adult industry then you can invest some money in a DSLR or High quality webcam depending on the kind of videos you are shooting. If your videos are in a Good quality then they will be viewed by more users. But don't spend your savings on this, just make sure that you have lighting and something to mount your camera/phone on to begin with.
- **Computer and Internet:** This is easy. Almost everyone has a computer/laptop and a internet connection these days. So this wont be a problem I suppose.
- **A good webcam:** Make sure it's a webcam that can shoot in 4K resolution, you can use it to record clips and shows too.
- **Software to edit:** This is not needed to begin with if you have a MacBook, since it's built into them. It can also be found for free online. But as you get better, you will want more powerful software to do your editing, the adobe suite has tools for this. But for now, you just need to start producing.

Selling Homemade Porn – How to sell Amateur Porn

Best sites to sell homemade porn

Here is the list of best sites to sell your content on. You really should signup to **all of them**- the more networks you signup on the more money you will make. What you do is this:

1. Signup to them

2. Make a spreadsheet where you prioritize them (always start working with the ones that I list recommended or highly recommended)

3. When you produce something, you post it to every site at the same day - that way you optimize your income.

Selling Homemade Porn – How to sell Amateur Porn

- Chaturbate *(Highly Recommended)* : A market leader in the camming space, now also allows selling homemade porn videos. I would highly recommend you to start camming to make real money in the range of $5-10K/month. You can also sell your videos on chaturbate to your fans and loyal followers. Dont just stick to selling videos, rather become a camgirl to make real changes in your life. This is the best one on my list.

- OnlyFans *(Highly Recommended):* The best place to sell your content when you are offline. People can install an app or just use the website and pay a monthly fees to get access to your content. If you aren't using this service you are truly missing out!

- BongaCams **(Recommended)** : Although one of the biggest camming site but still used by camgirls to sell nudes to their thousands of followers. Selling porn clips will be a piece of cake.

- ManyVids : This is my favorite network as there are thousands of customers who are ready to buy your adult videos. Just signup and start selling your content to customers. Upload your homemade porn and customers will buy that. You can also take custom requests on this network. You can also sell skype shows.

- MyGirlVids: This is a new website in the market but they are growing at a rapid pace. They have some amazing features that other leading players don't offer. They have fingerprint technology to find and get your stolen content removed with ease. Also the payout is very good and higher than compared to others. If you are signing up on the recommended networks, then make sure you sign up on mygirlvids. Make sure to complete your profile and upload your videos for maximum sales.

Selling Homemade Porn – How to sell Amateur Porn

- Sidedaddy : A new site in the market but surely gaining a lot of traction. A beautiful interface, helpful support and thousands of paying customers. Their model percentage is also higher than their competitors. A must sign up for any girl thinking of selling her adult videos/clips or homemade porn.

- SpicyFind : Spicyfind is another great network that is growing exponentially. The quality of customers and also the models is exceptional. A must join for anyone trying to sell their clips.

- Iwantclips : This website gets millions of visitors each month and this is why this is the best network. After iwantclips, manyvids and youkandy, are other highly recommended networks. Almost all girls who sell on manyvids also sell the same clips on iwantclips as well. Just upload the same video this network as well if you want to double your adult video sales. (This is the best tip i can give you on selling porn videos online)

- Extralunchmoney; Biggest adult marketplace on the internet. Known and trusted by thousands. You can sell so many things here: Adult sex videos, Homemade porn videos, used panties, media , snapchat accounts and much more. You can also get paid for sexting here. Head over and signup now.

- Customs4u: As the name suggests, you take custom requests of customers and then complete them to make money. The best part is that you can also upload the same content on various other networks to get normal sales as well.

- ModelCentro: Its a fanclub. People can access your content for a monthly fees. The only problem here is that you need a prior fanbase to get people to pay a monthly fees for your content.

Selling Homemade Porn – How to sell Amateur Porn

So now that's out the way, I hope you managed to signup to everyone. If it's too daunting, make sure you at least signup to Chaturbate, OnlyFans and BongaCams.

PRO TIP: **There is a new site out called AdultNode.com - it works like Facebook, Twitter and Instagram in one. Signup (it's free) and start posting teasers there, you can sell content, grow a following and use it to grow a following.**

Selling Homemade Porn – How to sell Amateur Porn

I have a free gift for you all. (actually only for serious people who really want to make money)

Make your profile on Chaturbate , AdultNode.com and OnlyFans and send me profile links (all three) and then I will do a **free profile review** for you. But to be eligible, you need to add 3 videos, 5 photos, profile pic, and bio for me to review, without it I can't write a review on your profile. When you've done this, send me a mail to hi@miketriumph.com- put in the title: Profile Review (e-book).

I also know the owners of AdultNode so I made a deal with them, if you put a link to your AdultNode profile in your Chaturbate or OnlyFans profile, they will give you 3 months free VIP account. That's a **GREAT way to grow your following** fast as those profiles get recommended to new users that signup to the service.

Make sure you mention that you put the link in the e-mail, that way I can get the VIP awarded.

Will my identity be revealed?

All the adult networks, sites make sure to protect your identity. But make sure that your "stagename" is not something that can identify you. Also consider choosing a different state/country than you live in.

You can geo-block the location you are in, so that people from that geographical location wont be able to find you and check your profile.

How to protect myself from people who steal my content ?

This has been a big problem in adult industry , specifically in camming industry. Pirates are just such a big nuisance. You can't control the data scraping but can make it bit difficult for pirates.

There are couple to ways to protect yourself. Either the camming network or the adult site where you upload content or perform will take care of DMCA complaints and getting your content removed from the internet. Or you can also file a DMCA complaint for searching for your content yourself.

You can also watermark your content for added protection. You can also use a service like Cam model protection (google it) as well. This is the only way to protect your online content.

You can also create videos where you blur our your face, it's possible and can sell - but it's harder and requires more work. It's up to you and what you are comfortable with.

Selling Homemade Porn – How to sell Amateur Porn

Advantages of selling your own adult porn clips/videos/pictures apart from webcam shows:

1. **This is extra income:** If you treat yourself as an established webcam model and that is your primary source of income, then branching yourself will help you earn even more money.
2. **Price of your content is set by you:** No need to work on predefined prices, set the price on the clips which you think it should be. Keeping it lower might increase sales, but higher prices generally shows that the content is premium content.
3. **Helps in creating a brand for yourself:** Creates an authority and an income stream that can generate money for YEARS to come.
4. **No need to trade time for money:** One of the biggest disadvantage of making money as a camming adult performer is that you need to maintain a schedule and also be very strict about it. A consistent schedule helps in making a loyal audience for the cam girl. When you start selling your clips, you can generate money when you aren't online - but you really need to do both. Your fans will want to interact with you.

Selling Homemade Porn – How to sell Amateur Porn

Best network/websites for selling adult porn video clips/pic etc?

Again another commonly asked question. Everyone wants to know the name of the network that is the highest quality in all the aspects.

But honestly I cannot give one name. Each network has its own advantages/disadvantages. You will have to check them out yourself, and make a decision. I can just guide you the once that I know people make the most money on.

Apart from being a webcam model, you can also make money selling your pictures, clips etc. There are many established websites to help you achieve this. I already gave you the list further above, so stop worry about what site to work on and just get started ;)

So what kind of content should I make?

It depends entirely on who you are and your situation. There is a huge difference between a 40+ year old MILF and a 18 year old Teenage girl and the audience for their content. If you are a guy or a girl, a couple, a transsexual - it doesn't matter. **There is a market!**

TRUST ME ON THAT ONE. There is someone out there that will want to see you naked, perform sexual acts and get off. Even if you look in the mirror and don't like what you see, there is someone that will love you on camera. Online or not.

What is most important is that you get started, make some videos. Post them. Have fun, you need to enjoy yourself - otherwise, what is the point? Don't pretend to be a star - be engaging with people and always respond when someone reaches out to you.

I have given you the best websites there is to work with. I don't want to go into detail about camera and lighting - because you need to get started and also any gear I point you to, will be obsolete in a few years anyways - this book will not.

So be sure to follow what I outline, do the work and you will start to see an income.

Selling Homemade Porn – How to sell Amateur Porn

1. **Use all platforms:** I cannot stress enough on how important is to sell the same content on all the recommended networks on this article.
2. **Survey the network:** The best way to find the profitable niche to sell your clips is by surveying the networks. Look at what other popular girls are selling. Is there a shift in selling certain fetish, like taboo porn is highly popular these days so you will see almost all models to have made few taboo porn videos like stepbrother-stepsister etc.
3. **Complete your profile:** Make sure you add a high quality profile picture, write an seductive bio covering all the fetish you will be covering. Also add photos, tangible items that you sell like used panties, Amazon wishlist's etc

But how do I actually make the porn videos?

You take off your clothes in front of a rolling camera and get off in your favorite way. There. That's one in the bank. Then you repeat it and get better. How do you do that? You get online on Chaturbate/Bongacash and show people the clip - post it on AdultNode and ask people what they think, don't be shy, don't be cheap - give stuff away to begin with.

Ask the viewers to give their honest opinion, write it down and don't take shit personal. When you have asked 10-15 people for input (you can do it online, no need to ask your friends unless you have those kind of friends haha). Gather their input, see what they all agree on and incorporate that in the next video.

That is how you get better.

Selling Homemade Porn – How to sell Amateur Porn

To decide what you want to actually produce, you can also follow these steps.

Steps to find out what content to make:

- **Find a fetish or niche:** You need to first find a fetish that you will be comfortable in make and also something that is trending, so that you know you will have buyers.
- **Look at various porn clips online on that fetish:** Go to pornhub, xvideos etc and look at the videos in that niche. How are models talking, what kind of videos they are making, what toys they are using, amount of views, comments etc. You need to understand your niche properly in order to get amazing sales
- **Upload and optimize:** Add the right keywords when you upload the video. Make sure the description and thumbnail is enticing enough to make people interested. People love new girls and your first impression matters a lot. Make sure you upload on all recommended networks to get the maximum sales.
- **Replicate the process with your own twist:** After you know what to d, get inspired and make few videos of your own. Add your own style to it and upload on all recommended networks of this article. Ask for feedback, use the feedback to your own advantage. Get better. Practice, the more your produce the better you become.
- **Promote on Fetish communities:** Make a list of all forums, communities, twitter hashtag, facebook groups etc where your target customers are present and influence them to buy.

Now that you've made your video, time to upload it

Every site has their own guides on how to upload videos. So make sure you read them before you start. You should also consider editing your videos. Depending on what type of device you are using, Windows computer, Mac or just a smartphone, there are applications that are relatively easy to work with.

The easiest to use are Macbooks, they are made for this sort of thing - editing videos is a whole different ballgame that there are many lengthy books written about, so I really just recommend that you get started w.o. spend too much money on equipment and fancy programs.

Learn as you go and you can and will do fine.

I made a promise to you above, to help you review your content. I stick by it if you missed my promise, it's because you didn't read this book close enough and that's a shame. It's a short but very valuable book. It could mean the difference between you trading your time for money, and you being free to spend your time like you want, because the money comes in regardless.

You decide. In either case, I wish you all the best.

Go make some money!

Mike T.

You **ARE** what you do. **NOT** what you say you want to do.

You made it this far. Congratulations! Did you do as instructed? Did you get started? You won't make it if you don't put in the work.

You won't be a professional from the trying once or twice. For every hour of television you watch, you should be working on your dream for 3 hours.

I have helped many people achieve their dreams, but I have watched equally many fail. The difference? Perseverance. The ability to keep working when it's hard and appear to not yield any results.

If you stick with it, week after week, month after month you will get there. Decide on a number, when you get there celebrate.

My first number was $10k/month, what's yours? Tell me at www.miketriumph.com

www.ingramcontent.com/pod-product-compliance
Lightning Source LLC
Chambersburg PA
CBHW040312220526
45473CB00002B/639